NAZI AND ESOTERISM

The Occult as Fascination and Menace

By

Jack Stew Barretta

Table of Contents

Esoterism and Occultism in Nazism

Scholarship on esoteric worldviews and occult movements has gained increasing momentum in recent years, challenging traditional views of the occult as historically marginal and anti-modern. Much of this new research reveals significant aspects of esotericism that had been previously underappreciated while re-aligning historical assumptions and re-assessing the ambivalent vision of alternative modernities pursued by occult practitioners and theorists. One result of this process has been an ongoing revised appraisal of the history of occult and esoteric thought in modern Germany.

In particular, earlier notions of an 'occult influence' on Nazism, perennially popular among occultists themselves, have given way to more nuanced examinations of the complex interaction between esoteric groups and various representatives of Hitler's regime. Many central questions nonetheless remain unanswered: Why did a wide range of occultists succumb to the allure of Nazism, at least initially? What accounts for the conflicting responses by different Nazi agencies to esoteric organizations, ideas, and practices? What made the occult both an object of fascination and a perceived menace in the eyes of Nazi officials?

Such questions enter the controversial territory. Perspicacious critiques of occult thought from prominent cultural figures such as Theodor Adorno, Walter Benjamin, Ernst Bloch, and Thomas Mann have long suggested that the widespread interest in esoteric theories within German society helped pave the way for the rise of National Socialism. Subsequent historians have pointed to the role of obscure esoteric beliefs in shaping Adolf Hitler's early racial views, or the enthusiasm for certain occult tendencies on the part of Nazi leaders Heinrich Himmler, Alfred Rosenberg, and Rudolf Hess, among others. What has received little detailed scrutiny is the complicated evolution of Nazi perceptions of the occult and their concrete impact on esoteric groups and individuals. In light of the pronounced success of occult ideas in gaining adherents and admirers among a broad swathe of the German public during the Weimar era, this largely unexamined aspect of the history of Nazism merits further consideration.

Previous treatments of the convoluted relationship between esoteric ideas and Nazi realities have tended to reduce this intricate situation to one of two mutually incompatible but equally facile scenarios: either occultists and Nazis were aligned with one another at a fundamental level, or the hostilities between them drove both sides to revile each other.

Nazi perceptions of the esoteric as both threat and allure, both fascination and menace, derived from complex sources. Occult claims sometimes found a congenial hearing within Nazi ranks, whether in the form of 'cosmic ice' theories or esoteric lore about Atlantis and Aryans. Paradoxically, it was this very receptiveness toward the occult on the part of some Nazis that spurred other Nazis to adopt an uncompromising anti-esoteric stance. A further complicating factor stemmed from the fact that several of the more zealous Nazi opponents of occultism had come from occult backgrounds themselves. Last, esoteric spokespeople adopted contradictory strategies in accommodating their worldviews and institutions to the Nazi regime, highlighting a large area of ambiguous ideological overlap between occult principles and Nazi doctrines.

Esoteric approaches took a wide variety of forms in interwar Germany, the most readily identifiable being theosophy and its German offshoot anthroposophy. A small but notorious descendant of theosophy, the aggressively racist occult movement known as ariosophy, found a stronghold in Austria. Astrologers, clairvoyants, spiritualists, grail mystics, Rosicrucians, rune readers, and sundry other arcane tendencies rounded out the esoteric scene. The borders between these tendencies were conspicuously porous, and it was common for the same individual to identify with multiple occult beliefs and practices. At the same time, the far-flung esoteric milieu intersected significantly with two other prominent alternative currents, the counter-cultural *Lebensreform* or 'life reform' movement and right-wing *völkisch* circles. In terms of personnel, organization, and ideology, the degree of convergence among the occultist, *Lebensreform*, and *völkisch* camps strongly marked the modern German occult revival.

When the Nazis came to power in 1933, esoteric connections to *Lebensreform* and *völkisch* streams played a central role in both occultist perceptions of Nazism and in Nazi perceptions of occult movements. Some esoteric groups were able to draw on this background to curry favor with particular Nazi agencies. Thus, ariosophist links to the *völkisch* milieu made ariosophy more respectable in the eyes of some Nazis for a time, while anthroposophy's contributions to alternative education, holistic health care, and organic farming gained anthroposophists the support of Nazi *Lebensreform* advocates. Several theosophical currents tried a similar strategy, cultivating an image of themselves as reliable partners of the regime.

Because the initial reactions of prominent esoteric figures have sometimes been misrepresented, they are worth examining more closely. A recent account portrays several leading German theosophists as alternatives to *völkisch* occultism or as simply victims of the Nazis, overlooking their *völkisch* publications and pro-Nazi statements. A particularly striking example is Johannes Maria Verweyen, General Secretary of the

German Section of the Theosophical Society Adyar from 1928 to 1935.

In 1933 Verweyen defended Nazi Jewish policy against criticism from non-German theosophists, arguing that "the so-called persecution of the Jews is, in reality, persecution of socialism and communism," and portraying Nazi antisemitic measures as "a response to the persecution of non-Jews by Jews, to the predominance of Jews in theater, literature, commerce, and so forth."

In 1934 Verweyen attempted a synthesis between theosophy and Nazism, emphasizing their commonalities. He offered an esoteric justification of "racial differences" and published a series of articles which "glorified Hitler and National Socialism." Praising the Nazi "reconstruction of the nation" as the work of divine providence, he commended Hitler's "Christian spirit" and "living faith in God." Verweyen's efforts to appease the new regime were fruitless, and his Theosophical Society was banned in July 1937. He was arrested in 1941, after leaving the theosophical fold, and died of typhus in Bergen-Belsen in March 1945.

Other strands of theosophy were even more aggressive in establishing a pro-Nazi profile. Two noteworthy examples are the "Theosophical Brotherhood" founded by Hermann Rudolph in Leipzig, and the Theosophical Society headed by Hugo Vollrath, also based in Leipzig. Both groups had Nazi party members in their leadership and competed vigorously with one another for the favor of Nazi officials, presenting their version of theosophy as the appropriate vehicle for the spiritual renewal of the German nation and greeting the dawn of the Third Reich with great enthusiasm.

In 1933 Vollrath's Theosophical Society declared Hitler's new order to be "the will of God." Vollrath himself had been a member of the Nazi party since 1931. In 1936 Vollrath boasted of his contributions to integrating the theosophical movement into the Nazi state. In a letter to SS General Reinhard Heydrich, he proposed establishing a "department for theosophy, mysticism and related areas" in the *Reichskulturkammer*, the Nazi cultural apparatus.

Rudolph's "Theosophical Brotherhood" went further still, portraying theosophy as the fullest expression of Nazism's true goals and apotheosizing National Socialism as the glorious next step in spiritual evolution. Rudolph's 1933 and 1934 publications promoted Germany's religious mission to unify the Aryan peoples, and characterized the Theosophical Brotherhood as "the partner of the National Socialist Movement in the spiritual sphere." Indeed, according to Rudolph, "theosophical doctrines provide the ideological and religious foundation of National Socialism." Such effusive proclamations of support for Nazism did not mollify Nazi opponents of occultism. Vollrath's Theosophical Society was under surveillance from 1934 onward, and in February 1935 the Gestapo ordered Rudolph's publications confiscated and banned. Anti-esoteric Nazis saw such groups as especially dangerous precisely because of their outspokenly pro-Nazi stance: by attempting to mix their doctrines with Nazi teachings, these theosophists threatened the ideological integrity of National Socialism. Both groups were dissolved in July 1937.

A similar fate befell other occult organizations, large and small. The spiritualist Weissenberg movement, founded by Joseph Weissenberg in the first decade of the twentieth century, preached spiritual healing and combined *völkisch* elements with theosophical components. By the 1930s its membership numbered in the tens of thousands. It was banned in January 1935. The "Association for Occult Science," with a total of 28 members, was dissolved in March 1935, while an esoteric group called the "League of Fighters for Faith and Truth" (*Bund der Kämpfer für Glaube und Wahrheit*) was banned in August 1935. The *Gottesbund Tanatra* was dissolved in July 1936, the "Study Circle for Psychic Research" was prohibited in January 1937, and the "New Salem movement" was banned in May 1937. Even the sizeable Anthroposophical Society, whose members enjoyed extensive protection from Rudolf Hess's staff and other Nazi party agencies, was dissolved in November 1935.

Other occult groups experienced the same treatment. The *Deutsche Neugeistbewegung*, a German offshoot of the New Thought movement, originated as a split-off from the Theosophical Society and exemplified the conjunction of occult and *Lebensreform* themes, promoting yoga and vegetarianism in esoteric form. Although the group was emphatically pro-Nazi and its leadership made up largely of party members, it was spurned not only by the security services but even by Nazi 'life reform' organizations and was expelled from the authorized *Lebensreform* association in 1934. Nazi officials categorized the movement as an occultist sect. Its newspaper, *Die weiße Fahne*, was allowed to continue publishing until 1941, but security agents kept a close watch on the group's publications. With thousands of supporters, the *Neugeistbewegung* was regarded as a competitor to, rather than an ally of, Nazi efforts to appropriate and assimilate alternative spiritual tendencies. A ban on the group was prepared in 1938.

Another paradigmatic example of the fusion of esoteric, *völkisch*, and *Lebensreform* perspectives was the Mazdaznan movement, an important occult tendency with members in Switzerland, Austria, and elsewhere in Europe. Founded in the US in the 1890s and established in Germany in 1908, Mazdaznan combined vegetarianism and Aryan supremacy, propounding a religion of racial regeneration, of revitalized Aryan blood, and Germanic rebirth and renewal. Influenced by theosophy and with a marked 'life reform' emphasis, the Mazdaznan movement opposed racial mixing and preached a new Aryan race of the future as well as a return to ancient Aryan values. This did not help its fortunes in the Third Reich. The Ministry of the Interior declared the Mazdaznan movement an enemy of the Nazi state in October 1935. Like other occult groups, its precepts were deemed incompatible with National Socialist doctrine.

What aroused the animosity of anti-esoteric Nazi officials was a perception that occultists represented an unusual peril, as a peculiar self-defined elite that was simultaneously aloof from the *Volksgemeinschaft* or national community while promoting worldviews that could be confused with Nazi ideals.

Esoteric groups were categorized as sects, marginal religious factions slated for elimination in the Nazi struggle against false idols. Occultists were additionally branded as bearers of internationalism, pacifism, and Jewish influence, and as organizationally affiliated with Freemasonry, a longstanding target of Nazi hostility. The anti-masonic image of 'occult lodges' became central to Nazi harassment of esoteric tendencies, and many occult groups were classified under the hybrid category of "Freemasonic, occultist and spiritualist sects." Tellingly, the most obsessive fascination with the occult was to be found among those Nazis who considered esotericism a grave threat to National Socialist principles.

Who were these committed Nazi opponents of occultism? In several prominent cases, they had esoteric affiliations of their own. The core of the party's anti-occult wing worked in the SD or *Sicherheitsdienst*, the intelligence arm of the SS. Some of its especially fervent collaborators had previously held a more welcoming view of esoteric approaches. Jakob Wilhelm Hauer, for example, cooperated frequently with the SD and offered workshops for Nazi cadre on "Occultism and its dangers for the Reich." He was a particularly fierce antagonist of anthroposophy, which he considered a dangerous rival to his religious organization, the German Faith Movement. Hauer's movement centered on a mixture of Nordic, neo-pagan, and Aryan elements and tried to rally the disparate *völkisch* religious factions under his leadership. He engaged in constant polemics against spiritual tendencies other than his own in an attempt to establish the hegemony of his idiosyncratic version of Aryan religious renewal. Thus, for Hauer, anthroposophy represented "a worldview that stood in the way of the religious goals of the German Faith Movement and must therefore be combated with all available means."

But Hauer's initial attitude toward anthroposophy was markedly more positive. Before coming to see it as a competitor to be eliminated, he approached anthroposophy as a potential ally and contributor to spiritual regeneration. In the early 1920s "Hauer saw anthroposophy as the beginning of a new era, an epoch of new and powerful intellectual and spiritual creation." He acknowledged the similarities between anthroposophy's esoteric framework and his aspirations: "Although Hauer emerged as one of the harshest critics of anthroposophy, he viewed anthroposophy at first as a spiritually related movement based on a foundation similar to his own, namely an answer to the spiritual desolation of the industrial age with all of its negative features." This changed as Hauer's religious ambitions grew: "From a perceived ally in the struggle for the spiritualization of life, anthroposophy quickly turned into a rival that had to be combated."

A similar development can be traced in the colorful career of SD employee Gregor Schwartz-Bostunitsch, a Russian émigré to Germany who had been an active theosophist and anthroposophist before transforming himself into an expert on the occult menace. Schwartz-Bostunitsch belonged to the Theosophical Society in Kiev in 1919 and embraced anthroposophy after moving to Germany in 1922. He was a dedicated anthroposophist throughout the 1920s until turning against anthroposophy in 1929. In 1930 he published a pamphlet attacking Rudolf Steiner, the deceased founder of anthroposophy, as an occult swindler and false prophet. Schwartz-Bostunitsch began as a public speaker for the Nazi party in Bavaria in 1923, met Himmler in 1924, and Hitler in 1925, and wrote for the flagship Nazi newspaper, the *Völkischer Beobachter*. He was officially named a Nazi party spokesman in 1927 and joined the SS in 1931. Though he had previously celebrated Steiner's work as a paragon of *völkisch* occultism, his attacks on anthroposophy became increasingly scurrilous in his capacity as an SD analyst of occult dangers after

1933. His elaborately conspiratorial reports eventually became so fantastic that Schwartz-Bostunitsch was forcibly retired by Heydrich, head of the SD, in 1937. Anthroposophists, for their part, denounced Schwartz-Bostunitsch as "un-German" and a "sinister Russian."

Before his acrimonious break with anthroposophy, Schwartz-Bostunitsch's mentor was the Swiss occultist Karl Heise, whose multifarious esoteric involvements exemplify the fluid borders between different occult sectors. Heise belonged to the Mazdaznan movement, was active in ariosophist circles, published widely in the theosophical and general occultist press, and was a member of the Anthroposophical Society from 1916 onward. He was a prolific author of conspiratorial texts in the years after World War I, including a 1919 book blaming the war on Western Freemasons and Jews, and a 1926 anti-masonic and antisemitic article published in Alfred Rosenberg's Nazi periodical *Der Weltkampf*. Heise's 1921 book on 'occult lodges' made an impression on Himmler, who read it in 1926 and praised it as "a deeply serious work." Heise's publications excoriated freemasons, occultists,

Jesuits, and Jews in Britain, France, Russia, and America for attempting to destroy Germany, giving particular emphasis to the notion of an occult-Jewish-masonic-Bolshevik conspiracy while extolling the true and healthy German occultism represented by Steiner. Thus, from an early stage, esoteric themes figured prominently in the volatile mix of ideas that eventually came to be turned, in Nazi hands, against esotericism. Both Heise and Schwartz-Bostunitsch contributed to the ideological groundwork upon which the SD's efforts against the occult menace were based.

Ostensible links between occultists and freemasons were crucial to Nazi measures intended to stamp out the perceived esoteric threat. Along with classifying occult groups as 'sects' and thus enemies of the vaunted national community, association with Masonic lodges carried dire implications. In internal directives, SD officers made clear that their eventual goal was "the destruction and elimination of all sects."

Freemasonry was viewed as an even more insidious enemy, at the very center of a shadowy realm of secret societies and international plots, pulling the strings of global events from behind the scenes. Masons appeared above all as the inevitable counterpart to 'world Jewry'; Hitler denounced the freemasons as an "instrument of Jewry" in *Mein Kampf*, and within the SD the sections for 'Freemasonry' and 'Jewry' were combined. For much of the 1930s, SD assessments of occultism were handled by the same staff who oversaw the anti-masonic campaign. Nazi attitudes toward freemasonry, in turn, revealed dynamics remarkably similar to those regarding occultism; substantial segments of the Masonic milieu displayed extensive ideological overlap with National Socialist thought, and not a few masons worked assiduously to accommodate themselves to the Third Reich. As with occultists, many German freemasons were simultaneous "victims and sympathizers of the National Socialist regime."

Making sense of the anti-esoteric obsession shared by parts of the Nazi security apparatus, and concurrent perceptions of the occult as both an object of fascination and a menacing adversary involves a closer look at the internal operations of the SD and its partners in the Gestapo, the 'secret police' of the Nazi state. The SD's fixation on occultism and other purported enemies of National Socialism can be traced in part to its uncertain status within the complicated Nazi bureaucracy. Founded in 1932 as a small intelligence service for the Nazi party, the SD struggled for years to establish a distinctive operational profile and an adequate budget for its activities, which included keeping tabs on friend and foe alike. As late as 1937, the SD remained "in search of image and mission."

The SD was not technically a police agency and did not have the authority to make arrests as the Gestapo did. Hence "the SD always seemed vulnerable to replacement by a more fully empowered and better-financed police force." This unstable situation generated a dynamic of simultaneous cooperation and competition between the SD and Gestapo, with the SD's role nominally confined to providing intelligence, research, and analysis. Structural factors such as these formed the background for the SD's exaggerated efforts to prove its indispensability to the Nazi cause.

Ongoing rivalry with the Gestapo also helped catalyze an escalating radicalization of the SD's expectations and standards. Nowhere was this more evident than in the branch of the SD devoted to *weltanschauliche Gegnerforschung* or 'research on ideological enemies' of Nazism, a term that became a key concept in the SD's arsenal. SD officers began to see themselves as experts trained in the authentic Nazi worldview, compiling information on the movement's assorted enemies.

In the process, SD analysts tended to overemphasize the supposed ideological divergence between their objects of surveillance and true National Socialist principles. Putative opponents of National Socialism "had to be portrayed as even more dangerous so that only the SD as ideological intelligence service [...] could be entrusted with defining and combating these enemies." The SD thus came to see Nazism as surrounded by invisible adversaries, working covertly – and in some cases even unconsciously – to undermine Nazism from within. Groups that seemed to share points of agreement with the Nazi worldview especially aroused the suspicions of the SD; such groups were considered even more dangerous than direct and open opponents of Nazism. All of this provided ample ammunition for Nazi officials in search of covert antagonists.

Esoteric individuals and organizations were merely one among many such targets, their status defined by broader Nazi priorities in combating alternative religious tendencies. The SD's enduring hostility toward occult groups and esoteric doctrines stemmed in part from the perceived organizational competition that such currents represented, but the anti-occultist faction of the SD viewed occult tendencies above all as an ideological threat to the integrity of the National Socialist worldview. In the eyes of the SD, occultists belonged, willingly or not, to the expansive panoply of *weltanschauliche Gegner* or ideological enemies of Nazism. The process by which this perception developed indicates that official Nazi hostility toward organized occult groups depended as much on underlying ideological similarity as on overt ideological distance. The SD's evaluation of a 1936 book on 'Aryan wisdom' provides a revealing example.

The book was authored by Ernst Issberner-Haldane, an ariosophist, astrologer, palm reader, an adherent of the *Neugeistbewegung*. In March 1936 an SS corporal named Nicolai in the SD's text analysis department in Leipzig submitted a report on Issberner-Haldane's book, characterizing its treatment of race as "dilettantish and pseudo-scientific." Nicolai's chief concern, however, was the ariosophical appropriation of Nazi themes. The report noted that Issberner-Haldane "repeatedly endorses the basic principles and actions of the National Socialist state in maintaining racial purity and eugenic health, which he amalgamates with his doctrine of reincarnation and perfection." Moreover, the ariosophist author "emphasizes somewhat ostentatiously his positive stance toward the National Socialist state" and presents himself as a "pioneer of the Aryan ideal, fulminating against the Jews as racially inferior." In Nicolai's judgment, however, Issberner-Haldane's book was "far removed" from the National Socialist worldview.

Nazi officials seem to have found ariosophical teachings embarrassing. Another 1936 SD report on ariosophy warned that its ornate racial mythology "offers especially suitable material for the international agitation against German race doctrine." The report concluded: "Ariosophist racial teachings consist of a series of untenable aberrations, making it necessary for the National Socialist state to distance itself sharply from this theory." The same analysis extended to theosophists and anthroposophists as well; SD evaluations depicted occult groups "such as the theosophical and anthroposophical associations" as a gathering place for surreptitious subversion of Nazi racial doctrine: "They attempt to give their endeavors a *völkisch* appearance and thus represent an acute danger to the ideological rectification of the German people." For the sake of ideological propriety, esoteric doctrines needed to be eradicated.

In this climate of suspicion, occultists were sometimes more than willing to endorse repressive measures against other occult groups. In a 1936 memorandum to Hermann Göring, leading anthroposophist Jürgen von Grone condemned theosophy and "Eastern occultism" – along with Freemasonry, liberalism, Marxism, Wall Street, the Jesuits, and the League of Nations – as enemies of the German spirit. He emphasized that the regime's suppression of "occult societies of foreign ethnic origin" was entirely justified, but that restrictions on anthroposophists were counter-productive, as anthroposophy was profoundly German and was actively combating the very same enemies as National Socialism. Grone also claimed that Nazism's foes, France, Britain, and Russia, were ruled by "occult brotherhoods" striving to destroy Germany. Supporters of anthroposophy in the Nazi hierarchy adopted a similar approach, arguing for lenient treatment of anthroposophists while condoning harsh measures against other occultists. An unsuccessful effort along these lines was initiated by high-ranking SS officer Otto Ohlendorf, a longtime sponsor of anthroposophist projects.

In May 1941 Ohlendorf proposed the immediate elimination of astrology, spiritualism, clairvoyance, and other un-German 'sects' which represented unhealthy Oriental forms of occultism. Anthroposophy, in contrast, called for more nuanced treatment, because of its deep German roots, its commitment to holism, and its connectedness to nature, all of which were of value to National Socialism. For anthroposophists and their Nazi supporters, Steiner's 'spiritual science' with its thoroughly German foundations decisively distinguished anthroposophy from its occult competitors and rendered it a fitting partner of National Socialist objectives.

None of these strategies served to placate the anti-esoteric faction. In a sense, such maneuvers infuriated SD specialists on 'ideological enemies' even more, aggravating their fears about the extent of support for occult activities within the party hierarchy. According to internal SD and Gestapo documents, esoteric initiatives enjoyed the backing not just of high-profile Nazis such as Hess and Ohlendorf but of Minister of Agriculture R. Walther Darré, 'Reich Advocate for the Landscape' Alwin Seifert, and Alfred Baeumler, head of the Office of Science on Rosenberg's staff, as well as lesser-known but influential figures like Interior Ministry official Lotar Eickhoff and Karl Heinz Hederich, director of the *Parteiamtliche Prüfungskommission zum Schutze des nationalsozialistischen Schrifttums*. Baeumler, for instance, displayed notable sympathy for anthroposophist undertakings such as Waldorf schools and biodynamic agriculture and provided positive assessments of Steiner's publications.

Baeumler's background in philosophy led him to appreciate the work of Steiner, who died eight years before the Nazis came to power and are sometimes considered "arguably the most historically and philosophically sophisticated spokesperson of the Esoteric Tradition." Steiner presented his teachings as an inclusive alternative worldview, a systematic approach offering answers to questions in all areas of life, and this ambitious undertaking won anthroposophy enthusiasts as well as enemies. Without endorsing Steiner's doctrines as a whole, Nazi leaders like Hess, Ohlendorf, and Baeumler considered specific aspects of anthroposophy, both ideological and practical, to be compatible with and complementary to National Socialist principles. While Ohlendorf was a consistent advocate for anthroposophist interests, Baeumler's attitude was more ambivalent. He was an ally of the Waldorf movement and supporter of biodynamic farming, but his analyses of anthroposophy's esoteric worldview combined praise and criticism.

From his position in the *Amt Rosenberg*, the agency which oversaw ideological education within the Nazi party, Baeumler commended the "deep and correct insights" underlying anthroposophy, but took exception to Steiner's teachings about race. This was a common theme in Nazi appraisals of esoteric thought; whether despite or because of the substantive commonalities between National Socialist and theosophically derived racial doctrines, occult treatments of race generally failed to find favor with Nazi observers. Nonetheless, Baeumler was considered a major protector of anthroposophy by its opponents as well as its proponents. He highlighted facets of "the philosophy of Rudolf Steiner" that were "valuable and worth adopting" into the Nazi worldview and the Nazi state.

Perhaps the most potent center of assistance for esoteric groups, in the SD's eyes, was the staff of Rudolf Hess, the Deputy of the Führer. Hess's occult predilections were a particular source of concern and object of scorn for Nazi foes of esotericism such as Heydrich, party leader Martin Bormann, and Propaganda Minister Joseph Goebbels. Hess was "profoundly interested in astrology, anthroposophy, the occult, and related areas." When Hess unexpectedly flew to Britain in May 1941, the anti-esoteric faction seized its chance to clean up the occult rabble once and for all. Goebbels scoffed that the letters Hess left behind explaining his enigmatic decision were "overflowing with half-baked occultism." The incident came at a delicate time for Nazi authorities, and the regime attempted to avoid embarrassment by blaming Hess's flight on occult influence. The ensuing jockeying for position and power in Hess's absence consolidated the standing of Heydrich, Goebbels, and Bormann. Four days after Hess's flight, Bormann sent a telegram to Heydrich reporting: "The Führer wishes that the strongest measures be directed against occultists, astrologists, medical quacks, and the like, who lead the people astray into stupidity and superstition."

The outcome was a coordinated operation against esoteric organizations, practices, and individuals across the Reich, officially dubbed the *Aktion gegen Geheimlehren und sogenannte Geheimwissenschaften* or "Campaign against occult doctrines and so-called occult sciences," supervised by the SD. Its aim was the definitive elimination of esotericism from the German national community. The campaign was launched on June 9, 1941, a month after Hess's flight to Britain and less than two weeks before Germany invaded the Soviet Union. Heydrich's initial order for the action was issued on June 4, with the arrests, searches, and interrogations to occur on June 9 between 7:00 and 9:00 AM throughout the Reich. The order applied to the entire expanded territory of the Reich, including Austria, Alsace-Lorraine, Luxemburg, and the 'Protectorate' of Bohemia and Moravia, and referred specifically to ten different categories of esoteric tendencies, identified as "astrologers, occultists, spiritualists, adherents of occult theories of rays, soothsayers, faith healers, adherents of Christian science, anthroposophy, theosophy, and ariosophy." The latter three seem to have been a primary focus, but every conceivable variety of occultism was eventually encompassed in the campaign's spotlight; the targeted groups came to include graphologists, dowsers, mesmerists, practitioners of divination, and believers in pendulums, numerology, hollow earth theories, and others.

On June 6, 1941, the SD issued a detailed set of instructions for interrogation of arrested occultists. The eleven-page guidelines contained descriptions of each type of occultist, followed by questions to be asked in each case. Suspects were to be punished according to their level of participation in esoteric activities, ranging from release on probation with a stern warning and permanent prohibition on future occult activities to internment in a concentration camp. Upon release, all suspects were to be sworn to secrecy regarding the action itself. The instructions for dealing with occultist publishers were notably harsh: All copies of occult publications were to be immediately confiscated, including inspections of printing shops, bookstores, and warehouses, as well as the business and personal quarters of all occult publishers, and correspondence with authors was to be impounded. The stated goal was "the complete elimination of all texts of this kind." Since the aim of the action was to vanquish 'ideological enemies' and put an end to 'occult doctrines,' the institutional basis for disseminating such doctrines had to be destroyed.

Finally, the SD distributed specific reports on several hundred individuals to be charged with "occult activities," providing details on those ostensible activities as well as recommended penalties for each person arrested. In many cases, the suggested measures were house search, interrogation, and police warning, as well as confiscation of correspondence in exceptional circumstances. Many other occultists were to be placed in investigative custody or arrested and imprisoned. One of the harsher examples is Caroline Thun, listed simply as a "Wahrsagerin," a fortune-teller or soothsayer; the recommended action in her case was "arrest and transferal to a concentration camp." Occultist publisher Karl Rohm, a fierce critic of anthroposophy, ariosophy, and other competing esoteric doctrines, faced serious penalties as well. He was to be sent to a concentration camp "for a long time" and have all of his property confiscated. One estimate puts the total number of arrests between 300 and 1000.

With occult organizations dismantled and esotericists under tight supervision, and with attention shifted to the new war in the East, the "Campaign against occult doctrines and so-called occult sciences" wound down in the summer of 1941. While the campaign largely removed organized esoteric activities from public view, occultism remained a focus of the Nazi struggle against 'ideological enemies' even after 1941, with ongoing efforts by the SD and others to keep the esoteric threat at bay. The propensity of occult groups to cast their elaborate spiritual precepts as the ideological foundation upon which a consistent Aryan or German viewpoint could arise, and to posit National Socialism as the political expression and practical realization of such a vision, caused consternation among skeptical Nazi observers. In their eyes, esoteric worldviews reversed the proper relationship between National Socialism and the occult aspirations that gravitated toward it: Nazism alone could serve as the underlying or overarching philosophy, not some conspicuously similar spiritual blueprint. Merely celebrating the Third Reich as a grand stage in the unfolding of cosmic-racial evolution was insufficient.

What made occultism into an 'ideological enemy,' in other words, was not so much ideological distance as ideological proximity. The SD discerned a menacing potential in the esoteric discourse on themes central to Nazism's self-understanding, above all on the intertwined topics of nation and race. What the SD feared was any prospective challenge to the hegemony of strict National Socialist teachings as they defined them, especially from currents that shared significant theoretical overlap with Nazi imagery and ideals. In an important sense, the point of *weltanschauliche Gegnerforschung* was to construct its targets and its objects of study, to create a profile of occultist tendencies and shape an image of the enemy into the mold prepared for it, and then mobilize against this invented opponent. Closer attention to the dynamics that gave rise to this process makes possible a more differentiated understanding of the mutually reinforcing perceptions and misperceptions which animated occultism's conflicted, ambivalent and imbalanced relationship to the Nazi state.

The widespread impression of some sort of connection between National Socialism and the occult, both considered to lie at the outer limits of historical comprehension, feeds the suspicion that there must be a hidden link between the two. But the links were neither concealed nor surprising. They can be explained not through the apparent deviance and strangeness of esotericism, but its commonness and popularity, through its participation in and influence by central cultural currents of the era. The consoling thought of both Nazism and occultism as eruptions of irrationality, as little more than a counterfeit of modern reason and social progress, depends on a simplified view of a complex history; it forgets that "the myths which fell victim to the

Enlightenment were themselves its products." This dialectical intertwinement of myth and enlightenment is central to the seemingly unusual manner in which the relationship between occultism and Nazism unfolded. Recognizing the multifaceted nature of this relationship can help to comprehend both its development in the Nazi era and its implications for today.

The history of occultism in the Third Reich can be viewed as a pivotal moment in a broader contest between esoteric hopes and political possibilities, allowing us to assess occultism as a historical subject in its own right rather than an easily dismissed oddity, a peripheral and fleeting phase from a bygone era, or a mysterious object of speculation and fantasy.

The Swastika

In antiquity, the swastika was a universal symbol, being used from the Bronze Age onwards on objects of every kind. The word 'swastika' comes from the Sanskrit: su (Greek eu, meaning 'good'), asti (Greek esto, meaning 'to be'), and the suffix ka. The symbol means 'good luck' (the Sanskrit-Tibetan word Swasti means 'may it be auspicious').

The shape of the swastika derives from the constellation Arktos, also known as the Great Bear, the Plough, and the Big Dipper. To the observer in the Northern Hemisphere, this constellation appears to rotate around Polaris, the Pole Star (an effect caused by the rotation of the Earth). If the positions of Arktos about Polaris are represented in pictorial form (corresponding to the four seasons), the result is highly suggestive of a swastika; in 4000 BC, they were identical to the symbol. It is for this reason that the swastika (aside from denoting good fortune) has been used to represent the Pole. The swastika gained in importance in European culture in the nineteenth century, primarily in the fields of comparative ethnology and Oriental studies. The absence of the symbol from Egypt, Chaldea, Assyria, and Phoenicia led the ethnologists to believe that the swastika was an Aryan sun-symbol.

The swastika appears in two forms: left-handed and right-handed. However, confusion quickly arises when one is faced with the question of how to define 'left' and 'right' concerning this symbol. Some occultists and historians favor a definition based on the direction taken by the arms as they extend outward from the center; while others prefer to define left' and 'right' in terms of the apparent direction of rotation. The confusion arises from the fact that a swastika whose arms proceed to the left appears to be rotating to the right, and vice versa. Each swastika variant has been taken to mean different things by writers on the occult, such as the Frenchman Andre Brissaud who says that the counter-clockwise-spinning swastika represents the rotation of the Earth on its axis and is the 'Wheel of the Golden Sun', symbolizing creation, evolution, and fertility. The clockwise-spinning swastika is, according to Brissaud, the 'Wheel of the Black Sun', representing man's quest for power in opposition to Heaven. The Chilean diplomat, esotericist, and Hitler apologist Miguel Serrano, has another explanation of the left- and right-handed swastikas: the left-handed (clockwise-turning) symbol represents the migration of the ancient Aryan Race from its homeland at the North Pole, while the right-handed (counter-clockwise-turning) symbol - the one used by the Nazis - represents the destiny of the Aryans to return to their spiritual center at the South Pole. Swastika with arms extending to left, apparent rotation to right / Swastika with arms extending to the right, apparent rotation to left After informing us of the complexities attached to the interpretation of left- and righthanded swastikas,

Whatever the validity of these theories, the ancient decorative swastikas show no preference whatsoever for one type over the other. The place where the left-right distinction is supposed to be most significant is Tibet, where the swastika of the ancient Bon-Po religion points to the left, the Buddhist one to the right. Now it is true that the Bon-Pos perform ritual circumambulations counter-clockwise, the Buddhists clockwise, but almost all the Buddhist iconography shows left-handed swastikas, just like the ones on the Bon-Pos' ritual scepter, their equivalent of the Buddhist vajra. One can only say that the swastika should perhaps be left-handed if (as in Bon-Po) it denotes polar revolution, and right-handed if (as in Buddhism) it symbolizes the course of the sun. But the root of the problem is probably the inherent ambiguity of the symbol itself, which makes the left-handed swastika appear to be rotating to the right, and vice versa.

The swastika gained popularity among German anti-Semitic groups through the writings of Guido von List and Lanz von Liebenfels, who took the symbol of good fortune and universal harmony and used it to denote the unconquerable Germanic hero. As might be expected, the counter-clockwise orientation of the swastika used as a banner by the National Socialist German Workers' Party (NSDAP) has also aroused considerable controversy in the occult and esoteric circles.

When Hitler called for suggestions for a banner, all of the submissions included a swastika. The one Hitler finally chose had been designed by Dr. Friedrich Krohn, a dentist from Sternberg. However, the design incorporated a clockwise-turning swastika, symbolizing good fortune, harmony, and spirituality. Hitler decided to reverse the design, making the swastika counter-clockwise, symbolizing evil and black magic. Here again, we encounter the problem of defining what is a right-and left-handed swastika. Was the Nazi symbol right-handed (traditionally denoting good) or left-handed (denoting evil)? In one sense, the Nazi swastika could be said to be right-handed because the hooked arms extend to the right; conversely, it could be said to be left-handed, since the apparent rotation is counter-clockwise.

We can speculate that Hitler had chosen to reverse the cross because of the connotations of black magic and evil in Krohn's cross and to evoke the positive images of good luck, spiritual evolution, etc., for his fledgling party!'

This interpretation is almost certainly correct, for two reasons. Firstly, we must remember that Hitler himself had very little time for occult mumbo-jumbo, and was certainly not the practicing black magician many occultists claim him to have been; and secondly, the idea that Hitler considered himself 'evil' (as he would have had to have done to take the step of reversing a positive symbol to a negative

44

one), or that evil was an attractive concept for him is ridiculous.

One of the most terrifying and baffling aspects of Adolf Hitler is that he did not consider himself 'evil'. Hitler was convinced of his rectitude, that he was acting correctly in exterminating the Jews and the other groups targeted for destruction by the Nazis. Also, Hitler himself makes no mention of such an alteration in his repulsive Mein Kampf. Because he took most of the credit for the design himself, neglecting even to mention Krohn's name, he would surely have explained the reasons for his making such a fundamental alteration to the design of the NSDAP banner: ...

> I was obliged to reject without exception the numerous designs which poured in from the circles of the young movement ... I - as Leader - did not want to come out publicly at once with my design, since after all, another might produce one just as good or perhaps even better. A dentist from Starnberg [sic] did deliver a design that was not bad at all, and, incidentally, was quite close to my own, having only the one fault that a swastika with curved

legs was composed into a white disk I, meanwhile, after innumerable attempts, had laid down a final form; a flag with a red background, a white disk, and a black swastika in the middle. After long trials, I also found a definite proportion between the size of the flag and the size of the white disk, as well as the shape and thickness of the swastika.

The reader will notice that Hitler says the submission he received that was quite close to his own had only one fault: the swastika had curved legs. The major importance of the decision [was] - for a man who prided himself on being a thwarted artist of great merit - not some unidentified occultic myth, but rather balance and aesthetic value'.

Heinrich Himmler and the SS

Many writers on the occult have suggested that the notorious SS (Schutz Staffeln or Defence Squads) was actively engaged in black-magic rites designed to contact and enlist the aid of evil and immensely powerful trans-human powers, to secure the domination of the planet by the Third Reich. While conventional historians are contemptuous of this notion, it nevertheless holds some attraction for those struggling with the terrible mystery at the heart of Nazism, who have come to believe that only a supernatural explanation can shed light on the movement's origins and deeds.

Although volkisch occultists such as Guido von List and Lanz von Liebenfels undoubtedly contributed to the 'mythological mood of the Nazi era' (with its bizarre notions of prehistoric Aryan superhumans inhabiting vanished continents), 'they cannot be said to have directly influenced the actions of persons in positions of political power and responsibility'.

However, the one exception is a man named Karl Maria Wiligut (1866-1946), who exerted a profound influence upon Reichsfuhrer-SS Heinrich Himmler. Before turning our attention to the SS itself, therefore, we must pause to examine the life and thought of Wiligut, and the reasons for his intellectual hold over the leader of the most powerful organization in the Third Reich.

The Man Behind Himmler

Wiligut was born in Vienna into a military family and followed his grandfather and father into the Austrian army, joining the 99th Infantry at Mostar, Herzegovina in late 1884 and reaching the rank of captain by the time he was 37. Throughout his years in the army, he maintained his interest in literature and folklore, writing poetry with a distinctly nationalistic flavor. In 1903, a book of his poems entitled Seyfrieds Runen was published by Friedrich Schalk, who had also published Guido von List. Although his studies in mythology had led him to join a quasi-Masonic lodge called the Schlarraffia in 1889, Wiligut does not seem to have been active in the volkisch or Pan-German nationalist movements at this time.

During the First World War, Wiligut saw action against the Russians in the Carpathians and was later transferred to the Italian front; by the summer of 1917, he had reached the rank of colonel. Decorated for bravery and highly thought of by his superiors, Wiligut was discharged from the army in January 1919, after nearly 35 years of exemplary service. At around this time, the Viennese occult underground began to buzz with rumors concerning Wiligut and his alleged possession of an 'ancestral memory' that allowed him to recall the history of the Teutonic people back to the year 228,000 BC. According to Wiligut, his astonishing clairvoyant ability was the result of an uninterrupted family lineage extending thousands of years into the past. He claimed to have been initiated into the secrets of his family by his father in 1890.

The source of this information about Wiligut is Theodor Czepl, who knew of Wiligut through his occult connections in Vienna, which included Wiligut's cousin, Willy Thaler, and various members of the Order of the New Templars (ONT). Czepl paid several visits to Wiligut at his Salzburg home in the winter of 1920, and it was during these visits that Wiligut claimed that the Bible had been written in Germany and that the Germanic god Krist had been appropriated by Christianity.

According to Wiligut's view of prehistory, the Earth was originally lit by three suns and was inhabited by various mythological beings, including giants and dwarves. For many tens of thousands of years, the world was convulsed with warfare until Wiligut's ancestors, the Adler-Wiligoten, brought peace with the foundation of the 'second Boso culture' and the city of Arual-Joruvallas (Goslar, the chief shrine of ancient Germany) in 78,000 BC. The following millennia saw yet more conflicts involving various now-lost civilizations, until 12,500 BC when the religion of Krist was established. Three thousand years later, an opposing group of Wotanists challenged this hitherto universal Germanic faith and crucified the prophet of Krist, Baldur-Chrestos, who nevertheless managed to escape to Asia. The Wotanists destroyed Goslar in 1200 BC, forcing the followers of Krist to establish a new temple at Exsternsteine, near Detmold.

The Wiligut family itself was originally the result of a mating between the gods of air and water, and in later centuries fled from persecution at the hands of Charlemagne, first to the Faroe Islands and then to Russia. Wiligut claimed that his family line included such heroic Germanic figures as Armin the Cherusker and Wittukind.

It will be evident from this epic account of putative genealogy and family history that Wiligut's prehistorical speculations primarily served as a stage upon which he could project the experiences and importance of his ancestors.'

Wiligut's 'cross-eyed thesis' was based on a spurious amalgamation of genuine cultural traditions (such as those described in the Eddas) and Theosophical belief systems that have little or no provenance in the actual history of mythology. In Wiligut's view, the victimization of his family that had been going on for tens of thousands of years was continuing at the hands of the Catholic Church, the Freemasons, and the Jews, all of whom he held responsible for Germany's defeat in the First World War.

His already somewhat precarious mental health was further undermined when his infant son died, thus destroying the male line of the family. This placed a great strain on his relationship with his wife, Malwine, who in any event was not particularly impressed with his claims of prehistoric greatness for his family. His home life continued to deteriorate, until his violence, threats to kill Malwine and bizarre occult interests resulted in his being committed to the mental asylum at Salzburg in November 1924. Certified insane, he was confined there until 1927.

Despite this, Wiligut maintained contact with his colleagues in various occult circles, including the ONT and the Edda Society. Five years after his release from the asylum, Wiligut decided to move to Germany and settled in Munich. There he was feted by German occultists as a fount of priceless information on the remote and glorious history of the Germanic people. Wiligut's introduction to Heinrich Himmler came about through the former's friend Richard Anders, who had contributed to the Edda Society's Hagal magazine and who was now an officer in the SS. Himmler was greatly impressed with the old man's ancestral memory, which implied a racial purity going back much further than 1750 (the year to which SS recruits had to be able to prove their Aryan family history).

Wiligut joined the SS in September 1933, using the name 'Karl Maria Weisthor'. He was made head of the Department for Pre- and Early History in the SS Race and Settlement Main Office in Munich, where he was charged with the task of recording on paper the events he clairvoyantly recalled. His work met with the satisfaction of the Reichsfuhrer-SS, who promoted him to SS-Oberfuhrer (lieutenant-brigadier) in November 1934.

As if his ravings were not enough, Weisthor introduced Himmler to another occultist, a German crypto-historian and List Society member named Gunther Kirchhoff (1892- 1975) who believed in the existence of energy lines crossing the face of the Earth. Weisthor took it upon himself to forward many of Kirchhoff's essays and dissertations on the ancient Germanic tradition to Himmler, who gave instructions to the Ahnenerbe (the SS Association for Research and Teaching on Heredity) to study them. One such dissertation concerned a detailed survey undertaken by Kirchhoff and Weisthor in the region of the Murg Valley near Baden-Baden in the Black Forest. After exhaustively examining 'old half-timbered houses, architectural ornament (including sculpture, coats-of-arms, runes, and other symbols), crosses, inscriptions, and natural and man-made rock formations in the forest', the two occultists concluded that the region had been a prehistoric center of the Krist religion. Unfortunately for Kirchhoff, even the Ahnenerbe came to think of him as a crackpot who understood nothing of scholarly prehistorical research (quite an indictment, coming from that particular organization). When Kirchhoff accused them, along with the Catholic Church, of conspiring against him, the Ahnenerbe responded by describing his work as 'rubbish' and him as a 'fantasist of the worst kind'. Despite this, Himmler continued to instruct the Ahnenerbe to take seriously Kirchhoff's unscholarly rantings, until the outbreak of the Second World War forced him firmly into the background. Weisthor, on the other hand, would make one further important contribution to Himmler's SS.

While traveling through Westphalia during the Nazi electoral campaign of January 1933, Himmler was profoundly affected by the atmosphere of the region, with its romantic castles and the mist- (and myth-) shrouded Teutoburger Forest. After deciding to take over a castle for SS use, he returned to Westphalia in November and viewed the Wewelsburg castle, which he appropriated in August 1934 to turn it into an ideological-education college for SS officers.

Although at first belonging to the Race and Settlement Main Office, the Wewelsburg castle was placed under the control of Himmler's Personal Staff in February 1935. Himmler's view of the Wewelsburg castle was likely influenced by Weisthor's assertion that it 'was destined to become a magical German strongpoint in a future conflict between Europe and Asia'. Weisthor's inspiration for this prediction was a Westphalian legend regarding a titanic future battle between East and West. Himmler found this particularly interesting, given his conviction that a major confrontation between East and West was inevitable -even if it were still a century or more in the future. Also, it was Weisthor who influenced the development of SS ritual (which we shall examine later in this chapter) and who designed the SS Totenkopfring that symbolized membership of the order. The ring design was based on a death's head and included a swastika, the double sig-rune of the SS, and a hagall rune. In 1935, Weisthor moved to Berlin, where he joined the Reichsfuhrer-SS Personal Staff and continued to advise Himmler on all aspects of his Germanic pseudo-history. Eyewitnesses recollect that this was a period of great activity, during which Weisthor traveled widely, corresponded extensively, and oversaw numerous meetings.

Besides his involvement with the Wewelsburg castle and his land surveys in the Black Forest and elsewhere, Weisthor continued to produce examples of his family traditions such as the Halgarita mottoes, Germanic mantras designed to stimulate ancestral memory ... and the design for the SS Totenkopfring.' In recognition of his work, Weisthor was promoted to SS-Brigadefuhrer (brigadier) in Himmler's Personal Staff in September 1936. While in Berlin, Weisthor worked with the author and historian Otto Rahn (1904-1939), who had a profound interest in medieval Grail legends and the Cathar heresy.

In 1933, Rahn published a romantic historical work entitled Kreuzzug gegen den Gral (Crusade Against the Grail), which was a study of the Albigensian Crusade, a war between the Roman Catholic Church and the Cathars (or Albigensians), an ascetic religious sect that flourished in southern France in the twelfth and thirteenth centuries. The Cathars believed that the teachings of Christ had been corrupted by the Church -and, indeed, that Christ was exclusively a being of spirit who had never been incarnated in human form. This belief arose from their conviction that all matter was the creation of an evil deity opposed to God.

Thus, they claimed that the dead would not be physically resurrected (since the body was made of matter and hence evil) and that procreation itself was evil since it increased the amount of matter in the Universe and trapped souls in physicality. The Cathars were eventually destroyed by Catholic armies on the orders of Pope Innocent III in the first decade of the thirteenth century.

Catharism held a particular fascination and attraction for Himmler and other leading Nazis. 'After all, the very word "Cathar" means "pure," and purity -particularly of the blood as the physical embodiment of spiritual "goodness" - was an issue of prime importance to the SS.' Just as the Cathars had despised the materialism of the Catholic Church, so the Nazis despised Capitalism, which they equated with the 'excesses of the Jewish financiers that - they said - had brought the nation to ruin during the First World War and the depression that followed'.

The Cathar belief that the evil god who had created the material Universe was none other than Jehovah provided additional common ground with Nazi anti-Semitism. Ritual suicide was also practiced by the Cathars. Known as the endura, it involved either starving oneself to death, self-poisoning or strangulation by one's fellow Cathars.

Another interesting point about the Nazi fascination with Catharism is: The Cathars were fanatics, willing to die for their cause; sacrificing themselves to the Church's onslaught they enjoyed the always-enviable aura of spiritual underdogs. There was something madly beautiful in the way they were immolated on the stakes of the Inquisition, professing their faith and their hatred of Rome until the very end. The Nazis could identify with the Cathars: with their overall fanaticism, with their contempt for the way vital spiritual matters were commercialized (polluted) by the Establishment, and with their passion for 'purity'. It is perhaps inevitable that the Cathars should have made a sacrament out of suicide, for they must have known that their Quest was doomed to failure from the start.

They must have wished for death as a release from a corrupt and insensitive world; and it's entirely possible that, at the root of Nazism, lay a similar death wish. Hitler was surrounded by the suicides of his mistresses and contemplated it himself on at least one occasion before he pulled the trigger in Berlin in 1945. Himmler and other captured Nazi leaders killed themselves rather than permit the Allies to do the honors for them. ...

Like the Cathars whom they admired, the Nazis saw in suicide that consolation and release from the world of Satanic matter promised by this most cynical of Cathar sacraments. The thesis of Rahn's book was that the Cathar heresy and Grail legends constituted an ancient Gothic Gnostic religion that had been suppressed by the Catholic Church, beginning with the persecution of the Cathars and ending with the destruction of the Knights Templar a century later. From 1933, Rahn lived in Berlin and his book and his continued researches into Germanic history came to the attention of Himmler. In May 1935, Rahn joined Weisthor's staff, joining the SS less than a year later. In April 1936, he was promoted to the rank of SS-Unterscharfuhrer (NCO). His second book, Luzifers Hofgesinde (Lucifer's Servants), which was an account of his research trip to Iceland for the SS, was published in 1937. This was followed by four months of military service with the SS-Death's Head Division 'Oberbayern' at Dachau concentration camp, after which he was allowed to pursue his writing and research full time.

In February 1939, Rahn resigned from the SS for unknown reasons and subsequently died from exposure the following month while walking on the mountains near Kufstein. As with Rahn's resignation from the SS, the reasons for Weisthor leaving the organization are uncertain. One possible reason is that his health was badly failing; although he was given powerful drugs intended to maintain his mental faculties, they had serious side effects, including personality changes that resulted in heavy smoking and alcohol consumption. Also, at this time his psychological history -including his committal for insanity - which had been a closely guarded secret became known, causing considerable embarrassment to Himmler. In February 1939, Weisthor's staff were informed that he had retired because of poor health and that his office would be dissolved.

Although the old occultist was supported by the SS during the final years of his life, his influence on the Third Reich was at an end. He was given a home in Aufkirchen but found it to be too far away from Berlin and he moved to Goslar in May 1940.

When his accommodation was requisitioned for medical research in 1943, he moved again, this time to a small SS house in Carinthia where he spent the remainder of the war with his housekeeper, Elsa Baltrusch, a member of Himmler's Personal Staff. At the end of the war, he was sent by the British occupying forces to a refugee camp where he suffered a stroke. After their release, he and Baltrusch went first to his family home at Salzburg, and then to Baltrusch's family home at Arolsen. On 3 January 1946, his health finally gave out and he died in hospital.

Heinrich Himmler

The man who was so deeply impressed with the rantings of Wiligut, who would become most closely associated with the terror of the SS and an embodiment of evil second only to Adolf Hitler himself, was born in Munich on 7 October 1900. Himmler's father was the son of a police president and had been a tutor to the princes at the Bavarian court, and thus applied suitably authoritarian principles on his own family.

No doubt it would be going too far to see in the son's early interest in Teutonic sagas, criminology and military affairs the beginnings of his later development, but the family milieu, with its combination of "officialdom, police work, and teaching", manifestly had a lasting effect on him.'

Himmler was not blessed with a robust physical constitution, and this hampered his family's initial intention that he should become a farmer. Nevertheless, the idea of the noble peasant remained with him and heavily influenced his later ideology and plans for the SS. After serving very briefly at the end of the First World War, Himmler joined Hitler's NSDAP. In 1926 he met Margerete Boden, the daughter of a West Prussian landowning family, and married her two years later. A fine example of the Germanic type (tall, fair-haired and blue-eyed), she was also seven years older than Himmler and is said to have inspired his interest in alternative medicine such as herbalism and homeopathy.

Himmler was appointed head (Reichsfuhrer) of the SS on 6 January 1929. At that time the organization had barely 300 members, but such were Himmler's organizational skills that he increased its membership to over 50,000 in the next four years. In 1931 he established a special Security Service (SD) within the SS, which would oversee political intelligence. It was led by the psychopathic Reinhard Heydrich, 'the only top Nazi leader to fit the racial stereotype of being tall (six feet, three inches), blond, and blue-eyed'.

Himmler took control of the party's police functions in April 1934, and then took command of the Gestapo (Geheime Staatspolizei or Secret State Police). SS units were instrumental in Hitler's Blood Purge of 30 June 1934, which saw the end of the

Sturmabteilung (SA), the brown-shirted and sadistic militia of the early Nazi Party, and its chief, Ernst Rohm. Members of the SS were required to correspond to special racial criteria (tall, blond, blue-eyed) and had to be able to trace their Aryan ancestry at least as far back as the year 1750. Initially, the SS membership included approximately 44 percent from the working class; however, as its status increased following the Nazi rise to power, it attracted more members from the upper class. By 1937, the three major concentration camps in Germany were staffed by the SS Totenkopfverbande (Death's Head Units), and the following year saw the formation of the Verfugungstruppe (Action Groups), which numbered 200,000 and which later became the Waffen-SS (Military SS). By the end of 1938, SS membership had reached nearly 240,000, a figure that would later rise to approximately one million.

The aims of the enormous SS apparatus were ... comprehensive and concerned not so much with controlling the state as with becoming a state itself. The occupants of the chief positions in the SS developed step by step into the holders of power in an authentic 'collateral state', which gradually penetrated existing institutions, undermined them, and finally began to dissolve them. Fundamentally there was no sphere of public life upon which the SS did not make its competing demands: the economic, ideological, military, scientific, and technical spheres, as well as those of agrarian and population policies, legislation, and general administration.

This development found its most unmistakable expression in the hierarchy of the Senior SS and Police Commanders, especially in the Eastern zones; the considerable independence that Himmler's corps of leaders enjoyed vis-a-vis the civil or military administration was a working model for a shift of power planned for the whole area of the Greater German Reich after the war. This process received its initial impetus following the so-called Rohm Putsch, and it moved towards its completion after the attempted revolt of 20 July 1944. The SS now pushed its way into 'the center of the organizational fabric of the Wehrmacht', and Himmler, who had meanwhile also become Reich Minister of the Interior, now also became chief of the Replacement Army. On top of his many other functions he was thus in charge 'of all military transport, military censorship, the intelligence service, surveillance of the troops, the supply of food, clothing and pay to the troops, and care of the wounded'.

71

The Ahnenerbe and the Rituals of the SS

It has been said of Himmler many times that his personality was a curious mixture of rationality and fantasy: that his capacity for rational planning, the following of orders, and administrative detail existed alongside an idealist enthusiasm for utopianism, mysticism, and the occult. This combination of the quotidian and the fantastic led to Himmler's conception of the ultimate role of the SS: 'his black-uniformed troops would provide both the bloodstock of the future Aryan master-race and the ideological elite of an ever-expanding Greater Germanic Reich'.

From 1930, Himmler concentrated on the formulation of his plans for the SS, which included the establishment of the SS officers' college at the Wewelsburg Castle in 1933. Two years later, he established the Ahnenerbe with the Nazi pagan ideologue Richard Walther Darre. The Ahnenerbe was the Ancestral Heritage Research and Teaching Society and was initially an independent institute researching Germanic prehistory, archaeology, and occult mysticism. It was subsequently incorporated into the SS in April 1940, with its staff holding SS rank. Levenda thinks it likely that the inspiration for the Ahnenerbe came from many German intellectuals and occultists who had subscribed to the theories of the volkisch writers of the late nineteenth century, as well as from the adventures of many explorers and archaeologists, including the world-famous Swedish explorer Sven Hedin.

Born in Stockholm in 1865, Hedin left Sweden at the age of twenty and sailed to Baku on the Caspian Sea. This was the first voyage of a man who would travel through most of Asia, and whose exploits would be recorded in the book My Life as an Explorer Hedin's voyages and tales of fabulous Asian cities did much to consolidate the European and American publics' fascination with the mysterious Orient - a fascination that had already been kindled by Madame Blavatsky and the Theosophical Society.

There is evidence to suggest that the Ahnenerbe itself was formed as a private institution by several friends and admirers of Sven Hedin, including Wolfram Sievers (who would later find justice at the Nuremberg Trials) and Dr. Friedrich Hielscher who, according to the records of the

Nuremberg Trial of November 1946, had been responsible for recruiting Sievers into the Ahnenerbe. There was a Sven Hedin Institute for Inner Asian Research in Munich that was part of the Ahnenerbe and as late as 1942 Hedin himself (then about seventy-seven years old) was in friendly communication with such important Ahnenerbe personnel as Dr. Ernst Schafer from his residence in Stockholm. Moreover, on January 16, 1943, the Sven Hedin Institute for Inner Asian (i.e. Mongolian) Research and Expeditions was formally inaugurated in Munich with 'great pomp,' a ceremony at which Hedin was in attendance as he was awarded an honorary doctorate for the occasion.

Hedin may have met Karl Haushofer while in the Far East since Hedin was an occasional ambassador for the Swedish Government and Haushofer was a German military attache. 'Given Haushofer's excessive interest in political geography and his establishment of the Deutsche Akademie all over Asia (including China and India, Hedin's old stomping grounds), it would be odd if the two hadn't met.'

Indeed, the Deutsche Akademie and the Ahnenerbe, whose director was Wolfram Sievers, were run along very similar lines. Dr. Walther Wust, the Humanities chairman of the Ahnenerbe who carried the SS rank of Oberfuhrer, was also acting president of the Deutsche Akademie. Both organizations conducted field research at Dachau concentration camp.

Himmler's vision of the SS required its transformation from Hitler's bodyguard to a pagan religious order with virtually complete autonomy, answerable only to the Fuhrer himself. As we have seen, Himmler chose as the headquarters for his order the castle of Wewelsburg, near Paderborn in Westphalia and close to the stone monument known as the Exsternsteine where the Teutonic hero Arminius was said to have battled the Romans. The focal point of Wewelsburg, evidently owing much to the legend of King Arthur and the Knights of the Round Table was a great dining hall with an oaken table to seat twelve picked from the senior Gruppenfuhrers. The walls were to be adorned with their coats of arms; although a high proportion lacked these -as of course did Himmler himself - they were assisted in the drafting of designs by Professor Diebitsch and experts from the Ahnenerbe.

Beneath the dining hall was a circular room with a shallow depression reached by three stone steps (symbolizing the three Reichs). In this place of the dead, the coat of arms of the deceased 'Knight' of the SS would be ceremonially burned. Each member of Himmler's Inner Circle of Twelve had his room, which was dedicated to an Aryan ancestor. Himmler's quarters were dedicated to King Heinrich I, the Saxon king who had battled Hungarians and Slavs and of whom Himmler was convinced he was the reincarnation, although he also claimed to have had conversations with Heinrich's ghost at night.

Inside the dining hall, Himmler and his Inner Circle would perform various occult exercises, which included attempts to communicate with the spirits of dead Teutons and efforts to influence the mind of a person in the next room through the concentration of willpower. There was no place for Christianity in the SS, and members were actively encouraged to break with the Church. New religious ceremonies were developed to take the place of Christian ones; for instance, a winter solstice ceremony was designed to replace Christmas (starting in 1939 the word 'Christmas' was forbidden to appear in any official SS document), and another ceremony for the summer solstice. Gifts were to be given at the summer solstice ceremony rather than at the winter solstice ... (A possible, though by no means documented, cause for this switch of gift-giving to the summer solstice is the death of Hitler's mother on the winter solstice and all the grief and complex emotions this event represented for Hitler. Understandably, Hitler - as the Fuhrer and at least nominally in charge of the direction the new state religion would take - would have wanted to remove every vestige of 'Christmas' from the pagan winter solstice festival. As a means of denying his grief? Or as an act of defiance against the God whose birth is celebrated on that day, a god who robbed Hitler of his beloved mother? It's worthwhile to note in this context that for a national 'Day of the German Mother' Hitler chose his own mother's birthday.)

Besides Christmas, weddings and christenings were also replaced by pagan rituals, and pagan myths, as we saw earlier in this chapter, influenced Himmler's choice of Wewelsburg as the SS-order castle. The meticulous work of Peter Levenda in unearthing previously unpublished documents from the period allows us to consider the pagan world view of the Ahnenerbe and the SS. The files of the Ahnenerbe contained an article by A. E. Muller originally published in a monthly journal called Lower Saxony in 1903, which describes the celebration of the summer solstice at the Exsternsteine monument near the Wewelsburg in the mid-nineteenth century. [They are] like giants from a prehistoric world which, during the furious creation of the Earth, were placed there by God as eternal monuments ... Many of our Volk is known to have preserved the pagan belief and its rituals, and I remember that some sixty years ago, in my earliest childhood days ... the custom was to undertake a long, continuous journey that lasted for whole days and which only ended on St John's Day, to see those ancient 'Holy Stones' and to celebrate there, with the sunrise, the Festival of the Summer Solstice.

The town of Paderborn itself also had considerable pagan significance, as demonstrated by a letter from a man named von Motz to the head of the Ahnenerbe, Wolfram Sievers, which is quoted in

Levenda's hugely informative book Unholy Alliance: I am sending to you now ... six photographs with explanatory text. Maybe these can appear in one of the next issues of [the official SS magazine] Schwarze Korps to show that it is to some extent a favored practice of the church on images of its saints and so forth to illustrate the defeat of adversaries by [having them] step on them.

The referenced essay also mentioned that there are depictions of the serpent's head, as the symbol of original sin, being stepped on [by the saints]. These depictions are quite uncommonly prevalent. It is always Mary who treads on original sin. Now, these pictures appear to be particularly interesting because the serpent refers to an ancient symbol of Germanic belief. At the Battle of Hastings, the flag of the Saxons shows a golden serpent on a blue field ...

The Mary Statue at Paderborn was erected in the middle of the past century in the courtyard of the former Jesuit College. As professor Alois Fuchs related several times before in lectures concerning the Paderborn art monuments, the artist that created the Mary Statue must have been a Protestant. This is for me completely proven because the face in the moon-sickle in every case represents Luther. It is well known that Rome and Judah, preferring thus to take advantage of their victims, created victory monuments for them.

These motifs are common in the volkisch underpinnings of Nazism, with the serpent, thought of as an archetype of evil in Christianity, considered sacred by the Aryans. Also, 'Rome and Judah shamelessly exploited the suffering of their people by depicting them as heroes or as vanquishers of evil through their agonies (thus reinforcing weak, non-Aryan suicidal tendencies among the oppressed populations of Europe).'

As we have noted, the Ahnenerbe received its official status within the SS in 1940, and while other occult-oriented groups such as the Freemasons, the Theosophists, and the Hermetic Order of the Golden Dawn were being suppressed, the Ahnenerbe was given free rein to pursue its line of mystical and occult inquiry, with the express purpose of proving the historical validity of Nazi paganism. Its more than 50 sections covering every aspect of occultism and paganism, including Celtic studies, the rituals surrounding the Exsternsteine monument,

Scandinavian mythology, runic symbolism, the World Ice Theory of Hans Horbiger (which will be discussed in Chapter Seven), and an archaeological research group that attempted to prove the geographical ubiquity of the ancient Aryan civilization.

Also, at the door of the Ahnenerbe must lie the ineradicable iniquity of the medical experiments conducted at Dachau and other concentration camps, since it was this organization that commissioned the unbelievably hideous program of 'scientific research' on living human subjects. The mental ambiguity of Heinrich Himmler - rational, obedient and desirous of security on the one hand; immersed in the spurious fantasy of Aryan destiny on the other - was demonstrated most powerfully in the final phase of the Nazi regime, when it became obvious that Germany would lose the war and the 'Thousand-year Reich' would become dust. From 1943 onward, Himmler maintained loose contacts with the Resistance Movement in Germany, and in the spring of 1945, he entered into secret negotiations with the World Jewish Congress. (By September 1944 he had already given orders for the murder of Jews to be halted, to offer a more 'presentable' face to the Allies, an order that was not followed).

Himmler's actions at this time indicate what Fest calls 'an almost incredible divorce from reality', one example being his suggestion to a representative of the World Jewish Congress that 'it is time you Jews and we National Socialists buried the hatchet'. He even assumed, in all seriousness, that he might lead a post-war Germany in an alliance with the West against the Soviet Union.

When the reality of the Third Reich's defeat finally overwhelmed his fantasies and sent them to oblivion, and the idea of disguise and escape finally presented itself to him, Himmler adopted perhaps the worst false identity he could have chosen: the uniform of a sergeant-major of the Secret Military Police, a division of the Gestapo. Such was his 'divorced from reality', even then, that it did not occur to him that any Gestapo member would be arrested on sight by the Allies. This indeed occurred on 21 May 1945. As their master, many SS men took their own lives in 1945, appalled less at Himmler's betrayal of Hitler through his attempts to negotiate with the Allies than at his betrayal of the SS itself and of the ideals that had given meaning (at least to them) to the destruction they had wrought upon their six million victims. The collapse of this SS ideal 'left only a senseless, filthy, barbaric murder industry, for which there could be no defense'.

Conclusion

Occultism is a curious and fecund beast. Beliefs, and the events to which they give rise, have a frequently unfortunate habit of generating additional beliefs. If, as in the case of Nazi occultism, the initial beliefs were little more than crypto-historical idiocies, there can be little hope of improvement in their ideological progeny. This book has been as much a history of belief about Nazi occultism as about Nazi occultism itself, and there is little doubt that the principal driving force behind the development of this belief is an attempt to explain the dreadful aberration that was the Third Reich.

Given that human beings have always been fascinated with the occult and the supernatural, precisely because they promise so much in offering the prospect of a higher meaning to the vagaries of existence, and given also our quest for an answer to the problem of evil, it is only to be expected that many should seek to explain Nazism in terms that transcend the merely human. We noted in the Introduction that some serious orthodox historians place Hitler outside the spectrum of human behavior

- a spectrum that includes the most barbarous of crimes. Hitler is seen by them as uniquely evil, wicked beyond even the human capacity for wickedness. Others, who are inclined to accept the reality of a cosmic evil originating beyond humanity, in some Outer Darkness eternally forsaken by God, see Hitler and the Nazis as examples of how, given the right circumstances, this Darkness can enter humanity, an 'eruption of demonism into history'.

Nevertheless, the demonic can easily be confused with insanity: one shudders to think of the number of unfortunates throughout history whose madness was mistaken by their fellows for possession by the forces of Darkness. We have seen that the origins of National Socialism can be traced to volkisch occultists who believed wholeheartedly not only in the existence of a prehistoric Germanic race of superhumans but also that their very superiority had been transmitted through the ages to modern Germans using a magically active, pure Aryan blood. The bizarre occult statements of Theosophists such as Madame Blavatsky, Rudolf Steiner, and others seemed to offer evidence of the existence of a fabulous Aryan race that established great civilizations on the lost continents of Atlantis, Lemuria, and the mythical island of Thule in the incredibly remote past. The idea of genuine Nazi occult power (as opposed to Nazi belief in that power) seems to have arisen out of our continuing fascination with the legends in which the volkisch and Pan-German occultists believed so fervently.

Belief in all aspects of the paranormal is extremely prevalent, whether it be a belief in alien visitation, the spirits of the dead, dark and demonic forces from beyond the realm of humanity, or technologically advanced prehistoric civilizations such as those of Atlantis and Lemuria; and it seems to me that this belief lies at the core of the mythological development of Nazi occultism that has occurred in the second half of the twentieth century. For if the supernatural exists, might not the Nazis have discovered a way to harness its power to further their dreadful ambitions? The answer to this question must be negative: we have already seen that the evidence for Hitler's initiation into the mysteries of the black arts is non-existent, while the evidence for his utter contempt for the mysticism of any kind (particularly that practiced by Himmler in Wewelsburg, his sick joke of a Grail castle) is documented time and again. Indeed, such as Hitler's lack of interest in these matters that he never deigned even to visit Wewelsburg. What of Himmler, then? Did he not practice dark rites with his SS Gruppenfuhrers in their Order Castle, attempting to contact the souls of long-departed Teutons? The answer to this question is, of course, yes.

However, occult-orientated writers have, over the years, continually made the same mistake in claiming that, because Himmler attempted to contact supernatural forces, those forces exist to be contacted. I consider myself a sceptic, rather than an incredulous doubter, and so I cannot say that supernatural forces do not exist, any more than I can say that they do exist. In truth, no one can. But we must not allow ourselves to make any connection whatsoever between Himmler's ideas on the supernatural and the veracity of the supernatural itself.

In their rise to power, Hitler and his Nazis were enveloped in an aura of mysticism almost despite themselves. This aura appears closer to the experience of occultism than any other major movement in the twentieth century. Hitler came to personify the invisible structure which became the occult myth dealt with here. With the help of contemporary occult writers, the illusion is today more pervasive.

We find no such occult mystique surrounding other aberrations of civilization...'

The aura of mysticism surrounding the Nazis was enhanced and disseminated throughout German society using photography and cinema, notably Leni Riefenstahl's virulently propagandist films, which include Triumph of the Will and Olympia, and which glorify German-ness and emphasize the inherent superiority of the Aryan race.

The Nazis were nothing if not masters of self-promotion.

Just as the early volkisch occultists took various elements of prehistoric mythology to construct a spurious history for the Germanic 'master race', so many occult-orientated writers have taken the image of the Nazi black magician and his diabolical allies and with it have attempted to create an equally spurious history of the Third Reich. The insubstantial edifice of their wild speculations is 'supported' by the incorporation of Eastern mysticism, with its tales of hidden cities inhabited by ascended masters who are the real controllers of humanity's destiny on Earth.

As we noted in the Introduction, with the passage of time and the deaths of important firsthand witnesses any chance of finding an adequate explanation of Nazism and the horrors it unleashed has now almost certainly been lost. We are left with the awful question that will continue to haunt us for as long as we remain human: why? The question is made more awful by the likelihood that the answer lies not in Outer Darkness, not in the 'Absolute Elsewhere', but much closer, in that most frightening and ill-explored of realms: the human mind.

CPSIA information can be obtained
at www.ICGtesting.com
Printed in the USA
BVHW072302291020
592123BV00014B/2056

9 781801 133470